D1487069

FREE TO BE ME

Photo credit : Tom Buck Photography

DOM & INK (Dominic Evans) is a freelance illustrator and merman based in London, England, from not-so-sunny Bolton (also in England), via Narnia. Growing up with a love of Buffy the Vampire Slayer, short shorts, and Starlight Express, Dom, like many others, struggled to fit in at school, in life, and mainly with himself. However, he soon found his voice through his passion for illustration and stories. This led him on a path to illustrate for large brands, stores, clients, and agencies.

He currently lives in east London and spends his time immersing himself in a graphic novel or an amazing book and then creating illustrations that he hopes will make your day and make you slay.

Also by DOM & INK:
Map My Heart: My Love Life in Doodles
Map My Style: My Fashion Life in Doodles

#FreeToBeMe

FREE TO BE ME

AN LGBTQ+ JOURNAL OF LOVE, PRIDE & FINDING YOUR INNER RAINBOW

DOM & INK

Penguin Workshop

To YOU, my lovely reader.
You inspire me and I haven't even met you yet.
Keep being brilliant.

PENGUIN WORKSHOP
An Imprint of Penguin Random House LLC, New York

Penguin supports copyright. Copyright fuels creativity, encourages diverse voices, promotes free speech, and creates a vibrant culture. Thank you for buying an authorized edition of this book and for complying with copyright laws by not reproducing, scanning, or distributing any part of it in any form without permission. You are supporting writers and allowing Penguin to continue to publish books for every reader.

The publisher does not have any control over and does not assume any responsibility for author or third-party websites or their content.

Visit us online at www.penguinrandomhouse.com.

ISBN 9780593094679   10 9 8 7 6 5 4 3 2 1

THIS BOOK BELONGS TO:

Throughout these pages, you will never be judged. So no matter what part of your journey you are on and no matter what sexuality, gender, shape, or color you are . . .

THIS BOOK IS YOUR SAFE AND HAPPY PLACE.

Who is this book for?

It's for EVERYONE!
If you're an LGBTQ+ reader,
or you think you might be—perfect.
You've come to exactly the right
place. Not LGBTQ+? That's OK!
This book is for you, too. Read it,
'gram it, learn from it, support it,
gift it to someone who might
need it right now.

ON MY DAYS OFF,
I'M A MERMICORN

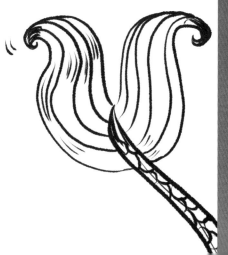

ME MYSELF AND HI

So here's me in a nutshell.

I'm Dominic. *Insert wave with large awkward hands* I grew up in Bolton in northwest England, where we have a really good Morrison's (that's a grocery store) and a great selection of charity shops (you call them thrift stores). My mum and dad are both from Manchester. Both worked in education while I was growing up, and both are lovely. Mum is hilarious, and very sassy and fierce, and Dad, while not a man of many words, finds the right things to say. My sister is awesome. She's seven years older, supersmart, and works a blond bob.

My parents raised my sister and me to be kind and thoughtful, and not to care what others think—although that last one can be hard for everyone.

I was bullied through primary and high school (you call that elementary and middle school). People made fun of me for how I sounded, what I wore, and the way I acted. In the early days of high school, I was constantly humiliated and made fun of. But you know what saved me from all of that stress and worry and annoying insecurities?
DRAWING.

And just look at me now, baby.

I'm a flipping mermicorn.

DOM &INK

THIS IS BASIC BETTY.*
SHE IS GOING TO ASK YOU
SOME REALLY SILLY
QUESTIONS IN THIS BOOK.
DON'T WORRY—SHE JUST DOESN'T
UNDERSTAND EVERYTHING YET!

BETTY!
STOP HAVING AN LGBTQ+
EXISTENTIAL CRISIS!
IT'S GONNA BE OKAY, HUN.

*JUST TO CLARIFY,
a "Basic Betty" could be anyone—
a coworker, fellow student,
or a misinformed friend.

CONTENTS

Chapter 1

OMG, LET'S BE FRIENDS!

YAS!

"Is this just a phase, then?"

This chapter is about getting you psyched and warmed up for the AMAZING JOURNEY AHEAD! You and me are gonna talk hobbies, friends, and gay dinosaurs. We're also going to touch on your family, friends, and BIGGEST supporters!

HUGS from DOM

RAINBOW ICONS

LIP-SYNC ON YOUR LUNCH BREAK!

LOOK for these badges throughout the book for empowering verbal hugs, inspirational public figures, and of course, lip-syncing and coloring in!

-3-

SAY CHEESE!

Draw or stick a photo of your
awesome self onto this
Polaroid frame:

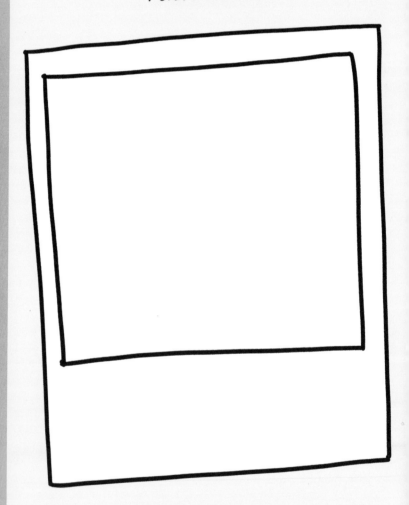

If you decide this drawing or photo
doesn't represent you in a year's
time, you can swap it out!

YOU'RE DOING Great!

HUGS from DOM

Scribbling about feelings or emotions can
be tough, so if it does get emosh at any point,
just head back to this page and look at
RILEY THE RAINBOW LLAMACORN
who doesn't give a fluff what others
think of them and is a total babe.

-5-

GETTING TO KNOW YOU

I need answers to these really very important questions.
THESE ARE DEAL-BREAKERS.
Color, write, or draw your answers!

YOUR FAVORITE GUILTY PLEASURE?

OR

TOP 3 HOBBIES?

YOUR FAVORITE BOOK?

YOUR NICKNAME?

WHICH FAMOUS PERSON INSPIRES YOU THE MOST?

FAVE ARTIST / BAND?

YOUR DREAM VACATION DESTINATION ON THIS POSTCARD:

Wish I Was Here...

COLOR THIS PACHYCEPHALOSAURUS ALL FANCY!

TITLE:

DIRECTOR:

NUMBER OF TIMES WATCHED:

BEST MOVIE EVER?

COLOR IN THIS DRAG QUEEN'S WIG WITH YOUR HAIR COLOR.

BEST TV SHOW EVER?

PERSON YOU CAN ALWAYS CALL?

-8-

RAINBOW ICONS

"I BELIEVE THAT MARRIAGE ISN'T BETWEEN A MAN AND WOMAN; BUT BETWEEN LOVE AND LOVE."

FRANK OCEAN is a Grammy Award—winning rapper, producer, and songwriter. In 2012, he posted an open letter on his Tumblr about his feelings for another man. Beyoncé and Jay-Z were among those who came forward to support him.

LIP-SYNC ON YOUR LUNCH BREAK!

Wherever you're having your lunch today, take a break, pull out some pens, put on your best dance track, and lip-sync away while coloring this FIERCE DRAG QUEEN!

-10-

Deep down, we're ALL mermicorns.
Draw yourself as one for me!

Cover this rainbow with colorful words about you, loving yourself, and how brilliant you are. ONLY POSITIVES ALLOWED.

FILL these boxes with daily affirmations to remind yourself that YOU GOT THIS, BABY!

I'M A FORCE OF NATURE!

I AM NOT LESS THAN ANYONE!

I CAN DO THIS!

Want some more affirmations? Why not try writing affirmations on sticky notes and use them to decorate your bedroom or notebook!

-15-

RAINBOW ICONS

"DIVERSITY IS STRENGTH. DIFFERENCE IS A TEACHER. FEAR difference, LEARN NOTHING."

HANNAH GADSBY is an Australian gay stand-up comedian. Her Netflix comedy special Nanette was met with critical acclaim. Basically, I want to be her friend. SO BAD.

YOUR SQUAD
Use ~~ONE~~ word to describe each
of these people in your life:

1. YOUR PARENT, CARETAKER, OR GUARDIAN
Trying her best

2. YOUR SIBLINGS
Innocent

3. YOUR BFF
All of the above?

4. YOUR ANNOYING COUSIN

5. YOUR PET ~~HAMSTER~~ Cat
IDK perfect

6. AUNTIE CAROL
Organic

7. YOUR TEACHER / BOSS
Funny

8. YOUR WORK / SCHOOL BFF
A lie

9. YOUR ROLE MODEL

10. YOUR SECRET CRUSH

11. THE MOST IMPORTANT—YOU
Incomplete?

Get ready—I'm coming in for a hug!
Draw yourself in this
MEGA AWESOME HUG-A-THON:

I SUPER NEEDED THAT HUG... THANKS, DOM!

HUGS from DOM

DON'T LIVE THE WRONG LIFE.

LIVE THE RIGHT ONE FOR YOU.

This lovely dinosaur, Brett, has a cute date tonight with a stegosaurus named Chad. Let's make him feel fabulous and color him in extra sassy. Say it with me now ... #SASSYSAURUS

YASSSSSS, BRETT!
WERK!

You should NEVER be scared of being yourself. Write down any worries you have on your mind on this page and the next.

Fill these boxes with random thoughts, anxieties, and concerns:

Finished? OK, GREAT.
Now yank this page OUT and tear
it to shreds. It's OK to be scared
but don't forget: YOU GOT THIS.

Chapter 2

FREE TO BE ME

"When did you choose to be gay?"

I want this chapter to be
a really positive experience
for you, just like the awesome
journey of exploring your
identity and sexuality should be.
If, for any reason, it doesn't
feel that way, that's OK.
Just fill in the exercises with
pencil. Opinions, attitudes,
and beliefs can change,
and time is a great healer.

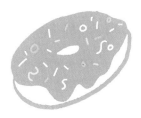

Now get ready to slay and
maybe eat a HUGE DOUGHNUT.
(I totally am right now.)

RAINBOW ICONS

"YOU are STRONG, YOU'RE A KELLY CLARKSON song, YOU GOT THIS."

JONATHAN VAN NESS is an American TV personality and grooming expert on the hit show Queer Eye. He is known for his gender-bending fashion, positive attitude, empowering quotes, and the most FABULOUS LONG HAIR. I love how he mixes humor with in-depth and thought-provoking one-liners.

The LGBTQ+ community is HUGE, DIVERSE, AND FULL OF LOVE. You've probably seen these letters before, so give 'em some popping color, baby!

 for LESBIAN

A homosexual woman who loves other women.

 for GAY

A homosexual man who loves other men. "Gay" is often also used as a term to refer to gay men and women.

 for BISEXUAL

A person who is attracted to more than one gender.

-27-

T for TRANSGENDER

Someone who identifies as
a gender different from the gender
they were assigned at birth.

Q for QUEER

An umbrella term for those who identify as L, G, B,
or T, but also people who fall beyond these labels. It
can also refer to anyone who prefers not to use the
traditional labels around gender or sexuality.

The LGBTQ+ community is HUGE! It's so awesome to live alongside so many inspiring and proud humans. You can use the glossary at the back of this book for further details on these terms!

A person born with biological characteristics of both sexes. Intersex people might identify as male, female, or non-binary.

INTERSEX

Someone who identifies as neither male nor female.

AGENDER

GENDERFLUID

A person who at any time or over time can identify as different genders.

-29-

NON-BINARY

Someone who identifies as a gender outside the binaries of male and female. Also known as genderqueer.

A person who has relationships with people regardless of their gender or gender identity.

PANSEXUAL

ASEXUAL

A person who is not sexually attracted to others.

-30-

DIVERSE BABES

Whatever your background, religion, race, sexuality, or gender, you have the right to BE who you are and to LOVE who you love. Give each of these huns a name and LGBTQ+ story:

Name:

Name: Angel

Name:

Story:
Born and raised in New York City, Angel spent their childhood feeling seperate from the people around them. They finally learned to be true to themself when their dad came out as transgender. This opened their eyes to a world

Story:

Story:

-31-

Name:

Story:

Name:

Story:

Name:

Story:

Name:

Story:

Name:

Story:

Name:

Story:

PRONOUN PARTY!

Color and decorate YOUR pronouns. If you don't see the pronouns that are right for you, fill in the speech bubbles and let me know!

SHE · HER · HERS

HE · HIM · HIS

THEY · THEM · THEIR

MAKING FRIENDS

Below are some new additions to your awesome squad. Alongside their name and gender, write their pronouns in the speech balloons:

Hi! I'm August and I identify as genderfluid. My pronouns are: she/they/it

My name is Cameron and I identify as a cisgender male. My pronouns are: he/they

Oh hai! I'm Shanice and I'm a trans woman. My pronouns are: she/her

If you don't want to misgender someone, just ask them which pronouns they use so they feel as comfortable as possible!

-34-

HOW ARE YOU SO EPIC?!

In this speech bubble, write down all the words that make you so EPIC!

PROUD FAITH

Your faith, sexuality, and gender should never be in conflict. No religion should ever make someone choose their faith over who they choose to BE and to LOVE. There are some fantastic LGBTQ+ groups out there for many different religions. Research them and write down your favorites here:

RAINBOW ICONS

"AS LONG AS YOU'RE SEEKING APPROVAL or VALIDATION THROUGH OTHER PEOPLE'S COMPLIMENTS or PEOPLE'S CRITICISMS, YOU'LL ALWAYS BE A VICTIM to WHAT OTHER PEOPLE SAY."

COURTNEY ACT is an Australian drag queen, pop singer, actress, and television personality. She was the first drag queen ever to win Celebrity Big Brother UK. Yas, queen. LITERALLY!

DRAW yourself as a superhero, as you're supercool. What powers would you have? Would you wear a shiny metallic leotard?*

*I would definitely wear a shiny metallic leotard.

-38-

COMING OUT

I remember the exact moment I realized I was gay.

These were the days before the jazz hands,
confident, and goofy Dom that I am now.
I was different. This was seventeen-year-old Dom.

I was walking through Manchester in my dungarees
and Timberland boots. Another lad my age crossed the
road toward me, and as he passed me, he said, "Hi."

I went bright red. I couldn't even move. I felt this huge
yearning to follow him, ask him about himself, what he
did, where he was from, and what his favorite Britney
Spears song was. I imagine it was "Oops," as "Toxic"
wasn't out yet and we all know that is THE ONE.

As time stood still in front of Marks & Spencer's
(a really popular store here in the UK), I thought to
myself, I think I'm gay. It's funny how so many people
add "think" or "kinda" in there, like you kind of sort of
know but you're trying to soften the blow to yourself.

That night, I decided to come out to my parents.

Yup. I was terrified.

I walked into the living room and sat down on
the couch. Mum and Dad were both chatting.
I think Mum was reading a magazine.

I said those words: "Mum, Dad—
I'm gay." Their faces lit up. A large disco ball
descended from the ceiling. The lights dimmed and
CHER, flanked by a gospel choir, entered the room
doing a really cute gospel version of "Believe."
A buffet was served, we all hugged, and then Cher
went home 'cause she was tired.

Unfortunately, this didn't happen. I won't ever forget
the long pause that came after I said I was gay.

It lasted long enough for me to
realize I had odd socks on.

"Right," my mum said.
Dad chipped in, "Why do you think that?"
The conversation went on till around 1 a.m. At the
time my parents were fifty-eight and sixty-eight,
respectively. They had me later on in life (good on 'em)
so, being older, I don't think they were as open-minded
as me. And it was clear that they were not happy.

My sister was called. She'd guessed from a young age
that I was gay, could not have cared less, and began an
amazing campaign of support and love that I don't
think I can ever repay her for. But she was at
university and far away. I didn't know
what to do and the heavy emptiness I felt
of being in our house, not accepted,
weighed me down daily, monthly, yearly.

-40-

(my sister. she's so sassy!)

I was very depressed, but I hid it well with jazz hands and funny jokes and bad highlights.

A few years later, I went to college, had boyfriends and experimented with guy liner (y'know, it DID look cute). The topic was rarely discussed with my parents again until 2014 when I moved back home to Bolton. I sat them down and we talked, and cried, and hugged.

They'd been fairly fine with my sexuality for a long time. It just hadn't been talked about. Looking back on the night I came out to them, it occurred to me that they had been just as scared about my future as I was.

The moment I realized that they had truly accepted me for ME was when they both agreed over Sunday dinner one day that I needed to meet a nice male accountant, mainly because I was shit at mathematics. I'm still thankful for that moment.

Still shit at mathematics, though.

16 x 4 - 3 = ?

ummm.

OUT OF THIS WORLD

It's a billion years in the future and an alien
has found the time capsule you buried!
It LISTS the five words that summarize
your LGBTQ+ journey so far . . .
What were they? WRITE them for me:

NAME:

1.
2.
3.
4.
5.

DATE:

translates from sassy alien
"This earthling is inspirational
and super awesome! When I get
my saucer license, I intend to
travel back in time so we can
be super fierce together!"

-42-

I'M SO FABULOUS I POOP RAINBOWS

SWEET TALK

ALL of us have days when we feel negative.
It sucks, BUT you have to remember
these crappy feelings will pass!
LEARN these positive affirmations for me so you
remind yourself DAILY of how fantastic you are:

1. I SHOULDN'T BE SO HARD ON MYSELF.
I'M TOO CUTE FOR THAT!

2. I KNOW ALL MY DREAMS CAN HAPPEN AND
I CAN'T WAIT TO SEE THEM IN 4-D!

3. THIS JOURNEY IS ONGOING AND I
SHOULD TAKE EACH DAY AS IT COMES!

4. I'M FRIENDS WITH A RAINBOW LLAMACORN.
THAT IS ALL.

5. I CANNOT PLEASE EVERYONE, BUT I
SHOULD ALWAYS STAY TRUE TO
MYSELF AND MY HEART!

6. TREAT EVERYONE WITH CARE, AND IF THEY
DON'T LIKE YOU, KILL 'EM WITH KINDNESS.

7. LOVE ALWAYS WINS. ALWAYS.

FOR EVERY PERSON WHO THINKS YOU'RE TOO FEMININE, TOO BUTCH, TOO SKINNY, TOO FAT, OR "NOT THEIR TYPE," THERE'S AT LEAST A MILLION OTHERS WHO THINK YOU'RE BEAUTIFUL.

Every journey is different. WRITE
a letter to yourself about your own
and how you rock the rainbow:

To:

PS - YOU ROCK

HUGS from DOM

YOU ARE SO BRILLIANT!

I'm your biggest fan, so I made you a sign.

Sometimes the journey across the rainbow might not go as planned. If things have ever gone wrong, WRITE down here what happened. Don't forget: I'm here for you.

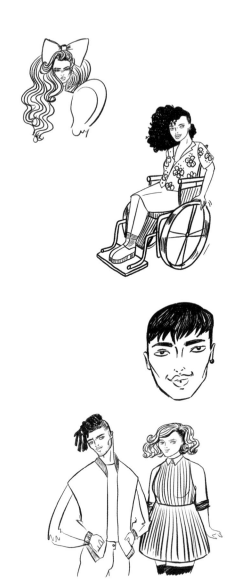

LOOK at all these amazing human beings who have come out to support you! They all understand how hard it is and how BRAVE you are.

LIP-SYNC ON YOUR LUNCH BREAK!

IT'S THAT TIME AGAIN . . . GRAB A HUGE DOUGHNUT, PUT YOUR FAVORITE TUNE ON, AND THEN COLOR IN THIS FABULOUS DRAG KING!

SHAPE UP

Scribble/collage/doodle in and around these shapes, showing me how you feel RIGHT NOW:

RAINBOW ICONS

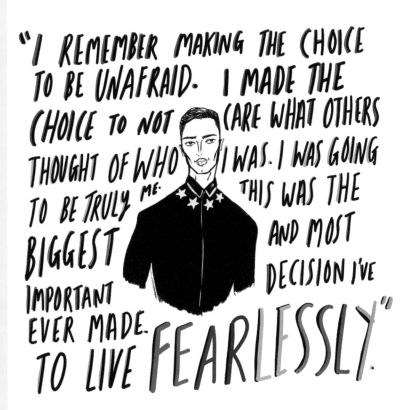

"I REMEMBER MAKING THE CHOICE TO BE UNAFRAID. I MADE THE CHOICE TO NOT CARE WHAT OTHERS THOUGHT OF WHO I WAS. I WAS GOING TO BE TRULY ME. THIS WAS THE BIGGEST AND MOST IMPORTANT DECISION I'VE EVER MADE. TO LIVE FEARLESSLY."

ADAM RIPPON is an American figure skater who won a bronze medal at the 2018 Winter Olympics. He is the FIRST openly gay US male athlete to win a medal.

On this page,
W R I T E
any negative things
people may have said
about you being YOU.

I don't want ANY NEGATIVE VIBES in this book so R I P and T E A R this page out! (Double-sided so you ain't missing out on anything.)

Trust me. You'll feel better for doing this!

HUGS from DOM

YOU ARE NOT ALONE

OMG, how CUTE are these
LGBTQ+ narwhals? I cannot DEAL.
Color them in, cut 'em out, and
stick them on your wall.

LOVE IS LOVE

RAINBOW ICONS

"ASKING WHO'S THE MAN AND WHO'S THE WOMAN IN A SAME-SEX RELATIONSHIP IS LIKE ASKING WHICH CHOPSTICK IS THE FORK."

chopsticks in love

ELLEN DeGENERES is a gay comedian, producer, LGBTQ+ activist, and talk-show host. OH MY GAWD, I LOVE HER.

DANCING QUEENS

COLOR IN THESE
STILETTO-STRUTTING BABES:

RAINBOW ICONS

"I NEVER REALLY think OF IT as COMING OUT as TRANS so MUCH as ENDING THE PRETENSE THAT I WAS A MAN. I DIDN'T reject MANHOOD I MORE EMBRACED WHO I REALLY was."

This is JUNO DAWSON. She is an author for young adults, the first-ever trans woman columnist for Glamour magazine and lover of a good animal print.

Throughout Juno's transition, I illustrated her.
Add some pattern and color to make this
doodle of her in 2015 POP.

JUST BE YOURSELF. NOTHING MORE.

What people don't tell you, and something I didn't realize, was that when you come out, you actually do it numerous times. In my head, I imagined that somehow, through telepathy, everyone else would sort of Know. But seventeen-year-old me was wrong. I had that conversation again and again.

While I had some support from friends and people at university, I also had really annoying responses like, "Well, we Kinda Knew" and "I always thought you woz gay."

WOW, great insight there from Basic Brian in my General Studies class.

BUT—I felt better for it.

Me using my gay telepathic superpowers

This hair was cool in 2004. HONEST.

However, this was 2004.
A fifteen-minute dial-up modem
was how I got online, and there was no one I knew
to ask about being gay. I was VERY lucky that my
friends were fine with it, but I'd still get random
whispers behind my back on the bus, people texting each
other across the table when I sat down, comments on
what I wore or how I sounded when I talked, teachers
giving me funny looks on days I felt more confident
with my double-denim ensemble (I looked fierce).

What people didn't know was that, behind my outgoing
persona, I was absolutely terrified. Anxiety hindered me
daily. Did I sound "too gay" in my presentation? Were
those people making fun of me? Was she still my friend?
Was I supposed to make a funny and sassy joke now?

If I could say one thing to seventeen-year-old Dominic,
it would be: "JUST BE YOU. NOTHING MORE."

I had a set idea in my head of how an out gay person
should act and I tried to become it—and you know what?
Just like the bootcut jeans I experimented with, it didn't
suit me. I was exaggerating parts of my personality
to fit an idea that wasn't really me, and it
took me a while to realize that.

STATUS UPDATE

What do you think you'll be doing in ten years' time? Fill in this list to show me. You can achieve ANYTHING, you know.

I LIVE IN: A decked out apartment in New York City

MY CAREER IS: An artist

MY NEW HOBBY IS: Making clothes?

MY UNICORN IS CALLED:

AUNTIE CAROL'S NEW NICKNAME FOR ME:

MY FAVORITE JUNK FOOD IS STILL:

MY FAVORITE MOVIE:

HUGS from DOM

YOU DESERVE all the LOVE

Chapter 3

FAM-ALLIES & FRIENDS

"I have a gay friend. Do you know her? Her name is Jenny."

In this chapter, we're celebrating your biggest cheerleaders. Fill this heart with the names of your rainbow crusaders!

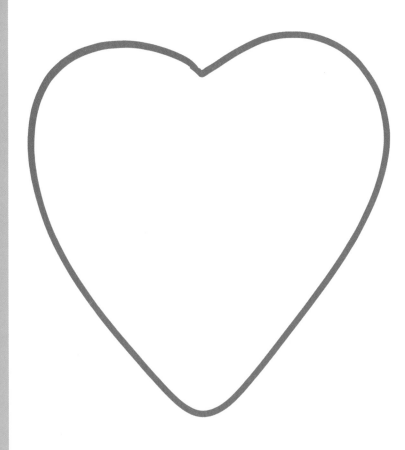

What is an ALLY?

An ally could be a straight or cisgender friend, relative, coworker, or Bob the PE teacher, who supports LGBTQ+ rights and loves and accepts you for YOU.

COLOR ME UP

Get your family and allies to write down all the ways you add color to their lives:

Feel better? GROUP HUG TIME!

SLAY THAT FACE

Carlos loves YouTube tutorials, comic books, dancing, and expressing himself with his creative and FLAWLESS makeup skills. Makeup ain't just for girls, people.

Using color, give Carlos on the LEFT a red-carpet-ready makeup look for his party tonight! Then ask an ally to color Carlos on the RIGHT, and see who creates the most sass-tastic face!

RAINBOW ICONS

"I LOVE the LGBTQ+ COMMUNITY MORE THAN I CAN SAY. SO I'LL ♫sing♫ ♫it♫ INSTEAD. FOREVER."

LADY GAGA is an award-winning bisexual singer, actress, songwriter, and LGBTQ+ activist. Her song "Born This Way" is a HUGE LGBTQ+ anthem about self-love, acceptance, and liberation of who you are! YAS GAGA!

It's Fred's first time at an LGBTQ+ rally and he wants to show his support! Get YOUR ally to think of and then write a slogan on the tee while you add some cute color:

HOW CUTE ARE THESE SHORTS?!

PARTY ON!

Your friends Malik and Samia have turned up at your door. They've got cake, fancy drinks, and a Spotify playlist. OMG, they're throwing you your own PRIDE party! YAS!

Here are some ideas for what your family and friends could do for you:

1. You need some amazing MUSIC. You know Auntie Carol will dance to anything.

2. Nice weather? Make a picnic! Maybe a cute game of Frisbee or football, too, if you're the sporty type?

3. DOUGHNUTS. PIZZA. CAKE. ALL THE SUGAR!

4. An empowering speech from your BIGGEST SUPPORTER to remind everyone why they LOVE you so much for WHO you are.

Please can Brett come? He's only just come out and wants to celebrate with you!

I'm so nice, I've even made you a poster.
I Know, right! Cut this out, color it in,
and stick it on your front door.

PRIDE
PARTY!

DISCO DROPPIN'

Grab your pens, friends, and fam, and
color in this dancing queen. If you can do
this dance move, too, then YA SLAY!

If you can't, that's OK.
I tried it once and split my jeans.

RAINBOW ICONS

"THE ONLY TIME THAT I REALLY CRIED DURING THIS WHOLE PROCESS IS WHEN I TOLD MY MOM AND SHE JUST SAID: 'ROBBIE, I DON'T CARE. WE LOVE YOU.'"

ROBBIE ROGERS is an American former soccer player. He came out in 2013 and was the first openly gay man to take part in a North American sports league when he played his first-ever match for the LA Galaxy.

-81-

GETTIN' GRATEFUL

Let your family, friends, and allies know you care. Here are some thank-you notes for you to cut out and pass around! I've left some blank for you, too . . . What will you write?

THANK YOU
for...

FROM:

TO:

TO:

FROM:

I APPRECIATE
THAT TIME YOU...

FROM:

RAINBOW ICONS

"IF YOU ARE BLACK, IF YOU ARE WHITE, IF YOU ARE STRAIGHT, IF YOU ARE TRANS GENDER- WHOEVER WHO-EVER YOU ARE, YOU WANNA BE, I SUPPORT YOU."

HARRY STYLES is an English singer, actor, and songwriter. He is very much an LGBTQ+ rights ally, sometimes even having the rainbow flag onstage as he sings his hits!

Time to chill. Color this repeat pattern of these adorable narwhals:

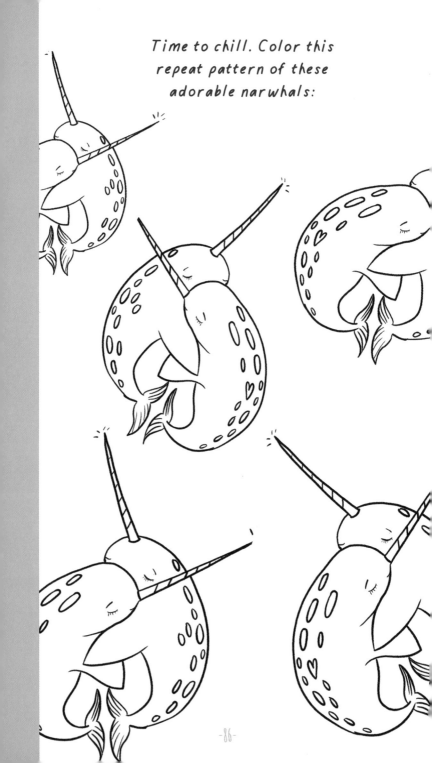

HUGS from DOM

Underline in bright pen the most important word on this page. Hint—it begins with "Y."

ONLY YOU DEFINE YOUR-SELF

PIN IT UP

Design some empowering LGBTQ+ pin
badges for your best ally to wear on their
brand-new black biker jacket! FIERCE!

HUGS from DOM

LOVE WHO YOU WANT TO...

Chapter 4

HATERS GONNA HATE

"Why are you
so camp?"

"Also, what is
camp?"

HOPEFULLY, YOU WILL NEVER HAVE TO DEAL WITH ANY KIND OF HOMOPHOBIA OR TRANSPHOBIA. IF YOU EVER DO, HERE ARE SOME HOT TIPS ON HOW TO GET THROUGH IT...

1. Stay calm. If you react, THEY WIN.

2. Always be the bigger person, as they can't be. WALK IT OFF.

3. Remind yourself you are an amazing rainbow narwhal and VERY FABULOUS.

4. If it's bad, TELL a parent/teacher/ friend and let them know what's happening.

5. If you need someone to talk to ASAP, call 1-866-488-7386, or go to www. thetrevorproject.org and chat with someone who can help.

Phoenix is heading into town, but they're nervous that someone might make fun of their AMAZING gender-bending outfit. COLOR in the outfit and FILL these speech bubbles with inspiring words!

FYI, Phoenix had the BEST time in town and found themself a cute handbag!

LATERS, HATERS!

Sometimes people might use hateful words against you, but this is THEIR ignorance and not YOURS. In these speech bubbles, write any words that have been said to you or you've heard, then COVER THEM IN LOTS OF GLITTER, BABY!

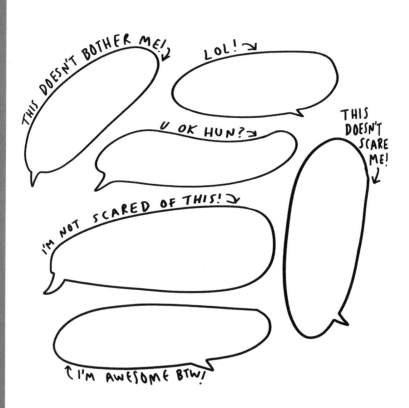

THIS DOESN'T BOTHER ME!

LOL!

U OK HUN?

THIS DOESN'T SCARE ME!

I'M NOT SCARED OF THIS!

I'M AWESOME BTW!

Look how sparkly they are. No need to be scared of these words now!

-94-

SLOGANS & SLOTHS

Serena the Rainbow Sloth gives NO SHITS about homophobia and has written these inspiring slogans for you! GET COLORING!

"RULE!"

I LOVE ME!

"MY HERO IS ME!"

NOT AFRAID!

I'M EMPOWERED

HUGS from DOM

AIN'T GOT NO TIME for HATE!

Write your own affirmation:

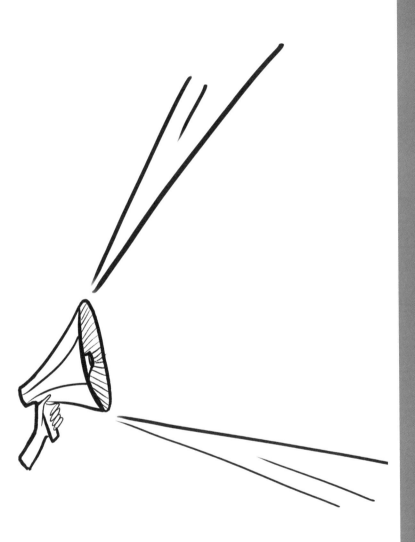

If you do buy a megaphone,
I personally think you
should cover it with glitter.

BREEZE THROUGH THE NEGATIVES...

Every journey is different! WRITE or DOODLE all your worries or anxieties in the boring gray smudge.

You shouldn't let these negatives weigh you down!
Go get some CAKE.

EMBRACE THE POSITIVES!

YAY! Now WRITE or DOODLE all the amazing positive things on your mind in this super-happy blue smudge!

These are the things
narrow-minded people see.

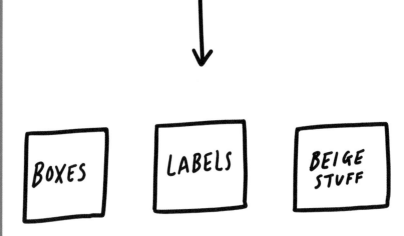

BOXES   LABELS   BEIGE STUFF

No one likes beige.
NO ONE.

*You're not narrow-minded, though.
You see explosions of color, love,
equality, and acceptance for everyone!
Scribble or draw whatever you like.
This page, like your mind, is limitless.*

YOU can LOVE who YOU want.

FRAME THIS PLEASE!

Add your own inspirational slogan
to each of these cute tees:

LIP-SYNC ON YOUR LUNCH BREAK!

Pick your best ANTHEM about self-love and empowerment. Turn up the volume, let your lip-sync skills flow, and your coloring game show! (OMG, I'm a POET!)

RAINBOW ICONS

"WE EXIST and YOU WILL NOT DIMINISH OUR LIGHT and BRILLIANCE."

JANET MOCK is a New York Times best-selling author, TV host, and trans activist. She SLAYS.

Color this, tear it out, fold it up, and stick it
inside your bag/purse/statement drag-queen clutch.

HUGS from DOM

BE YOUR OWN RAINBOW!

HUGS from DOM

ALWAYS KNOW YOUR OWN SELF-WORTH

RAINBOW ICONS

"THE THINGS THAT MAKE US DIFFERENT, THOSE ARE OUR SUPER POWERS."

LENA WAITHE is a screenwriter, actress, producer, AND my future best friend (she just doesn't know it yet). At the 2018 Met Gala she wore a RAINBOW CAPE on the red carpet. SHE IS ICONIC.

FLY HIGH!

Tyrese the pterodactyl is upset. The triceratops he likes (Dwayne—he's super shallow) has just told him he's not interested. He says Tyrese is too "skinny" and "girly" for him. WHAT A JERK.

Color Tyrese and write some words of comfort around him to remind him that it's about WHO you are deep down and he is AWESOME.

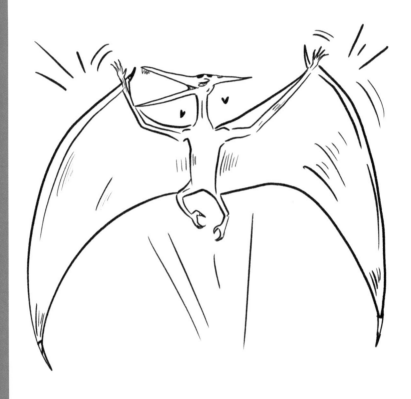

YAY! Tyrese feels so much better knowing
you got his back! Write some words
of empowerment around Tyrese as you both
fly off for PIZZA. YES, PIZZA.

SELF-CARE & SLOTHS

Serena the self-care sloth is back (though she needs you to add her rainbow stripes). When you need some YOU time, here are some LGBTQ+ self-care tips:

1. Be selfish. Do something that makes you HAPPY and fills your heart with joy. Mine is watching critically panned movies featuring dinosaurs or aliens. I love 'em.

2. Turn your phone OFF for a few hours. Escape social media, memes, and Auntie Carol's selfies. Have a digital detox and clear that brain out.

-111-

3. DO something physical. Go for a run with a friend or a walk. Take a dance class or play a sport. Get your body moving!

4. GET a haircut, buy them stilettos, splurge on that cap you wanted. Boost your self-confidence.

5. PICK UP THIS BOOK. Find a random page and fill it in. Coloring is very mindful, y'Know.

WRITE down what else you do for YOU:

Using pencil, write down what is
happening in your life right now:

Wait FIVE years (set a reminder on your
phone), now write down (in pencil again)
what has happened and is happening
in your life right now:

See how much has changed!

"MY MOM GAVE ME SOMETHING that HAS HELPED ME MY WHOLE LIFE. SHE SAID, 'IF IT DOESN'T MATTER IN FIVE YEARS, IT DOESN'T MATTER.'"

CHER NEEDS NO INTRODUCTION. SHE'S CHER, BITCHES!

Chapter 5

OVER THE RAINBOW

"But why isn't there a straight Pride?"

WOW.

What a journey. It's our final chapter and it's AMAZING. We're going to talk about Pride, LGBTQ+ icons throughout history, inclusivity within the community, and space rockets.

Yep. I said space rockets.

In between these rainbow lines, scribble down all the words that come to mind when you read the word "PRIDE."

HUGS from DOM

Any time life stresses you out, just look at this page and think about how much you've achieved . . .

I'M SO PROUD OF YOU

KNOW YOUR RIGHTS

Many campaigners and LGBTQ+ activists have come before us to fight for our equal rights. Here are ten (of MANY) events in LGBTQ+ history to know.

1 1924 – The first LGBT rights organization (the Society for Human Rights) is created by Henry Gerber in Chicago. Yas!

2 1951 – Roberta Cowell becomes the first known British trans woman to undergo gender reassignment surgery.

3 1969 – The Stonewall riots take place with members of the New York City LGBTQ+ community fighting against a police raid on the Stonewall Inn.

4 1970 – Marking the one-year anniversary of the Stonewall riots, the first Pride parade occurs in NYC. Now Pride events happen everywhere around the globe.

5 1980 – The largest civil rights organization in America is founded by Steve Endean: the Human Rights Campaign Fund.

6 1992 – Being gay is not a mental illness. Thankfully the World Health Organization officially declared this! However, the WHO only stops categorizing trans people as being mentally ill in 2018.

7 1993 – Minnesota passes the first legal protections for gender identity in all employment.

8 1994 – "Don't Ask, Don't Tell" is passed, barring gays, lesbians, and bisexuals from serving openly in the US military. It is repealed in 2011.

9 2015 – The US Supreme Court rules that the right to marry is guaranteed to all same-sex couples.

10 2018 – A court in India overturns a ruling from a 2013 judgment that upheld a colonial-era law that gay sex was illegal. That judgment was a huge breach of human rights, and India has officially recognized that gay sex is legal in their country.

KNOW YOUR ICONS

LGBTQ+ history is FULL of so many inspiring icons for you to learn and read about. Here are some who hold a special place in my heart.
Research each icon and write one line underneath about what you learned about them:

HOPE WILL *NEVER* BE SILENT.

HARVEY MILK
(May 1930–November 1978)

I AM DELIBERATE and afraid of NOTHING.

AUDRE LORDE
(February 1934–
November 1992)

THE REASON WE ARE SUCCESSFUL, DARLING? MY OVERALL CHARISMA, OF COURSE.

FREDDIE MERCURY
(September 1946–November 1991)

FRIGHTENED MEN BEHAVE AS IF THE TRUTH WERE NOT TRUE.

BAYARD RUSTIN
(March 1912–August 1987)

WHAT A COMFORT IS THIS JOURNAL...

ANNE LISTER
(April 1791–September 1840)

PAY IT NO MIND.

MARSHA P. JOHNSON
(August 1945–July 1992)

ADD AN ICON OF YOUR OWN AND DRAW/WRITE ABOUT THEM HERE:

DRAG IT UP!

Drag queens and Kings are performance artists who dress up (drag queens are usually men who dress as women, drag Kings are usually women who dress as men—though anyone can drag up, regardless of how they identify) to challenge gender norms, promote self-expression, and bring people together. The fierce queens below are LOVING Donna Summer and their gorgeous lace-front wigs. Add color, print, and patterns!

Add some volume to this queen's wig by listing the top five reasons why YOU think drag queens and Kings are important to the LGBTQ+ community:

OH, HONEY. YOU SLAY!

1.

2.

3.

4.

5.

RAINBOW ICONS

"BULLYING DID grind ME DOWN, BUT DRAG DID THE OPPOSITE. IT PROVIDED ME with confidence AND helped SHIELD SOME OF MY VULNERABILITY."

JAMIE CAMPBELL was banned from attending his school prom for wanting to attend in drag. He turned up in persona as FIFI LA TRUE and was welcomed by his friends, fellow students, and some awesome parents!

-127-

WERK, JOEY!

Joey is off to a school dance. His drag look still needs a wig, makeup, colors, and more! SASS HIM UP, BABY!

IF LOOKS COULD SLAY!

These queens are due onstage in five minutes but forgot their eye Kits! Add lashes, eyeshadow, and color to make 'em pop!

Smokey!

Comedy!

Disco!

Bored.

YAS, HONEY! These girls are ready to slay!

SISSY THAT PAGE

DRAW and create your drag persona in the star! Your drag name is your first pet's name and the first street you lived on ... Mine is "FIZZY GARDEN." WRITE your name in the scroll below the star! WERK IT, QUEEN.

BRING IT TO THE RUNWAY!

WERK!

YAS, QUEEN!

Lifestyle LOVIN'

Here are some tips on keeping
your life as rainbow-tastically
awesome as possible...

1. Don't rush anything—
whether that's dating
or parties or new friends.
Take your time.

2. Remember your self-worth?
Don't forget that.

3. Never put yourself in any
social or confrontational
situation you are NOT
comfortable in.

4. Don't judge others.
We've all had different paths
here, so remind yourself of
that when meeting others.

5. You don't have to be
liked by everyone!

6. Britney Spears is amazing.

7. If you're an ally reading this,
keep empowering those
LGBTQ+ people in your life!

8. YOU'RE BRILLIANT.
Have I mentioned how proud
I am of you?!

PRIDE

Pride events are held so that LGBTQ+ people can live their lives without prejudice or persecution. Through parades, demonstrations, rallies, and amazing dancing, Pride is a protest to raise awareness for equal rights for the LGBTQ+ community worldwide.

Add color to these Pride-ready babes:

The majority of Pride events happen in June (LGBT Pride Month in the US) to commemorate the Stonewall riots, which were a HUGE moment in LGBTQ+ history. COLOR the inn below:

In New York in the 1960s, police raids on gay bars were frequent. However, during the Stonewall Inn raid, tensions escalated and a full-on riot began, which carried on for several nights and sparked a number of LGBTQ+ activist groups to form.

Flash forward a few decades and the Stonewall Inn is now a recognized US national monument and also has an amazing nonprofit organization named after it.

PRIDE PROM

OMG, it's TOTALLY PROM NIGHT.
Remember these DIVERSE BABES from
earlier in the book? They don't have any
dates . . . yet. DRAW THEM!

Cut this out and stick it on your wall. You CAN party at Pride, but it needs to be with the intention of equal rights, inclusivity, and raising awareness for everyone!

HUGS from DOM

PRIDE IS A PROTEST NOT A PARTY

LET'S GET POLITICAL

You're off to a protest for equal rights.
Design your own sasstastic sign!

FIRED UP AND FABULOUS

Now, write or draw sign slogans for each of the topics I've left you. Spread those politically positive messages all around!

1. LGBTQ+ people of color!

2. Equal rights for trans people!

3. LGBTQ+ rights globally!

4. Equal rights for women!

5. More inclusivity in LGBTQ+ events!

6. Anti-racism within the LGBTQ+ community!

WOW YOU ARE SO AWESOME!

RAINBOW ICONS

"GAY COMES IN all different SHADES and COLORS, guess I'M PART of THE RAINBOW."

MNEK is a British singer and songwriter who has written for many big names like Beyoncé, Madonna, Kylie, and more. His lyrics narrate his experiences as a black, gay, proud man! His hair is always EPIC.

PRIVILEGE CHECK

The LGBTQ+ community is beautifully diverse; however, every person's journey and story is different and not every shade of the rainbow is fully represented, especially those who also suffer prejudice due to their race, faith, gender, or disability AS WELL as their sexuality.

For example, as a cisgender white gay man, my journey would be completely different from the journey of an Asian nonbinary disabled person.

It's important to "check" and be aware of our privilege so we can recognize other people's journeys and together help promote much wider representation in the LGBTQ+ community.

Fill in these exercises with pencil, because when it comes to privilege, we are always learning.

Have you ever been judged or bullied for something you could not change about yourself? Write about it here:

If you speak a second language, write "Hello" here:

If you feel you are not represented in the media enough, write down why, and how that can change:

Dyke marches are held across the world, are lesbian-led, and are held during Pride events but are focused on protesting. Cassie is on her way to one—add some color and draw an awesome squad to support her!

THIS IS WHO WE ARE. THIS IS WHO I AM.

Trans Pride events are held across the world!
Each of them is to promote the visibility
and activism of transgender, intersex, and
genderfluid members of the LGBTQ+ community.

TRANS RIGHTS ARE HUMAN RIGHTS

If you can't make it to a Pride
event, you can still show support.
Maybe make a poster to stick on
your bedroom wall during Pride Month!

RAINBOW ICONS

"I KNOW MY PERSPECTIVE SHOULD MATTER AS LONG AS I'M CONFIDENT and BEAUTIFUL."

AARON PHILIP is a nineteen-year-old disabled, genderfluid, teen model who has posed for a number of fashion shoots and promotes inclusivity in the LGBTQ+ community.

-146-

I really want to know who your dream crush is.
Because I'm super nosy.

Dream Crush!

OMG, HOW DID I NOT KNOW?!

HIT THE AISLE

Thirty countries (and counting!) have legalized same-sex marriage. That includes South Africa, the USA, Ireland, the UK, and most recently, Australia and Ecuador!
The Netherlands was the first country to legalize it in 2000. Now DECORATE YOUR FUTURE WEDDING CAKE!

P.S. Not everyone chooses to get married, which is fine, BUT if you do, I REALLY want to be a bridesman. PLEASE.

I'm a sucker for a good romance! Relationships these days take many different forms within the LGBTQ+ community. Write a LOVE STORY for how each of our couples met:

Trans woman Tareen
and cisgender man Furquan

Genderfluid Charlie and
cisgender woman Michela

Cisgender woman Ayana
and trans man Kaden

Cisgender gay men
Nick and Daniel

THEY'RE ALL SO CUTE I CANNOT DEAL!

FIND YOUR OWN PRIDE

Pride for many isn't just once a year. It's all year round. There are plenty of ways to rock your rainbow!

1. Start your own LGBTQ+ themed book club. Get a gang together, pick a great book, and discuss all the ideas and themes you read about.

2. Lots of movie-streaming services have their own LGBTQ+ category with films, TV shows, documentaries, and more for you to watch and enjoy!

3. Get creative! Write a story, or create some art that makes you PROUD. Go on—do me a little doodle on the canvas . . . you know you want to!

4. Show off your fashion skills and customize some clothes with dyes, make pin badges, or embroider that tee with some rainbow colors!

5. C'mon. I know you've been dying to get that Pride playlist on. Turn it UP!

6. Museums and galleries aross the world will be having plenty of themed exhibits for Pride season. Why not go and check them out?

HUGS *from* DOM

PLEASE NEVER STOP BEING YOU

FLY HIGH

You have a new addition to your superhero wardrobe. A CAPE! Color it in and draw yourself under it so you can soar to the skies!

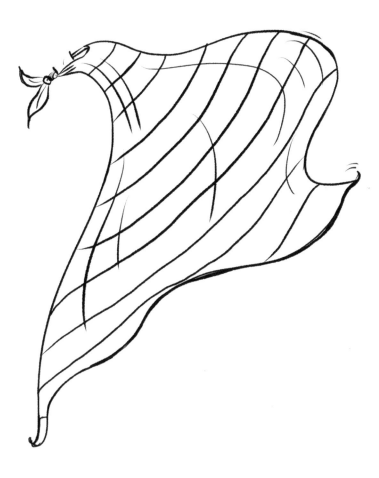

Planet Earth is MASSIVE and full of so many amazing people who will always love and accept you regardless of who you choose to love.

Cover this planet with color and glitter to spread happy vibes ACROSS THE WORLD!

SISSY THAT CROSSWALK

So many cities now have rainbow-painted crosswalks and pathways to show their citizens, tourists, and any curious UFOs that they support love for all! Color this crosswalk rainbow-style:

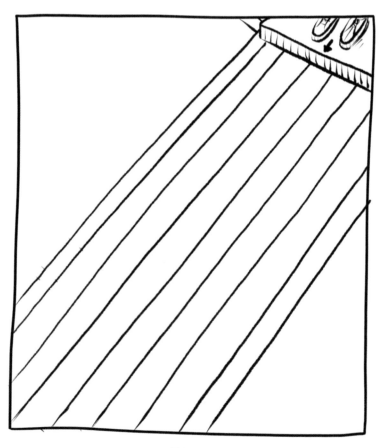

Write down all the things you are THANKFUL for right now:

HUGS from DOM

YOU are so EPIC

This repeat pattern of your
favorite drag queens needs
your immediate coloring attention:

LIP-SYNC ON YOUR LUNCH BREAK!

RAINBOW ICONS

"BE YOURSELF; EVERYONE ELSE IS TAKEN."

OSCAR WILDE was a queer Irish writer, playwright, and poet. He was known for his wit and sassy quips. This quote isn't a true quote of his, but he was so fabulous people think that he did say it!

Write three positive things about yourself
and your journey next to each letter.
Then cut this out and frame FOREVER.

P:
•
•
•

R:
•
•
•

O:
•
•
•

U

D

BLAST OFF!

Remember we said how cool Pride could be
in space? We've just been invited to
a Pride party on THE MOON. Yep, those aliens
are just as keen to party and dance to Britney
as we are ... Decorate this Pride rocket,
because we need to arrive in style, right?!

RAINBOW ICONS

"DON'T JUDGE US. WE ARE SIMPLY BEING OUR AUTHENTIC SELVES."

KENNY ETHAN JONES was the first transgender man in the world (!) to be part of a campaign to end the stigma around trans men having periods. WHAT A LEGEND!

OMG, BETTY!

You've listened to what we've put
into this book and you totally understand
the LGBTQ+ world now!
So when are we going for coffee?
Also, have you been getting
makeup tips from Carlos?

YOU LOOK
FABULOUS!

Oh dear. Judgy Jeff is approaching and he's making some phobic comments. However, Betty is gonna SASS HIS ASS outta here! What does she say?

YAS, BETTY! WERK!

Now grab your kitten heels and your purse, Betty. Auntie Carol's waiting at the karaoke bar. We're gonna go party, baby!

You will always be YOU.
And you've also got a HUGE
new supporter. ME.

Take a peek out of your window . . .
LOOK at all these amazing
LGBTQ+ people who have come
to show some love. As you COLOR
them in, don't forget, no matter
where you are on your journey,
there is always a community
and a family for you.

And
SO MUCH LOVE.

(And rainbow animals, obvs.)

FREE TO BE ME

And now it's time for goodbye. For now
at least, or until you next pick up this book.

I hope this has been a space for you to share
your story and journey. The more we share, the
more we empower and strengthen one another.

One thing that you should take from this book
is that you deserve it ALL. All the love,
all the support, all the hugs, all the dancing,
all the silly moments with family.
Because YOU are a champion.

And anytime you doubt that? PICK UP
THIS BOOK, because these pages will
always be your safe and happy place.

So, Auntie Carol and Betty are waiting at
Karaoke for us. Are you coming or what, hun?!

As I was writing this book, my mum sent me
a letter about her reaction to me coming out.
She doesn't usually open up a lot.
This is how the letter ended:

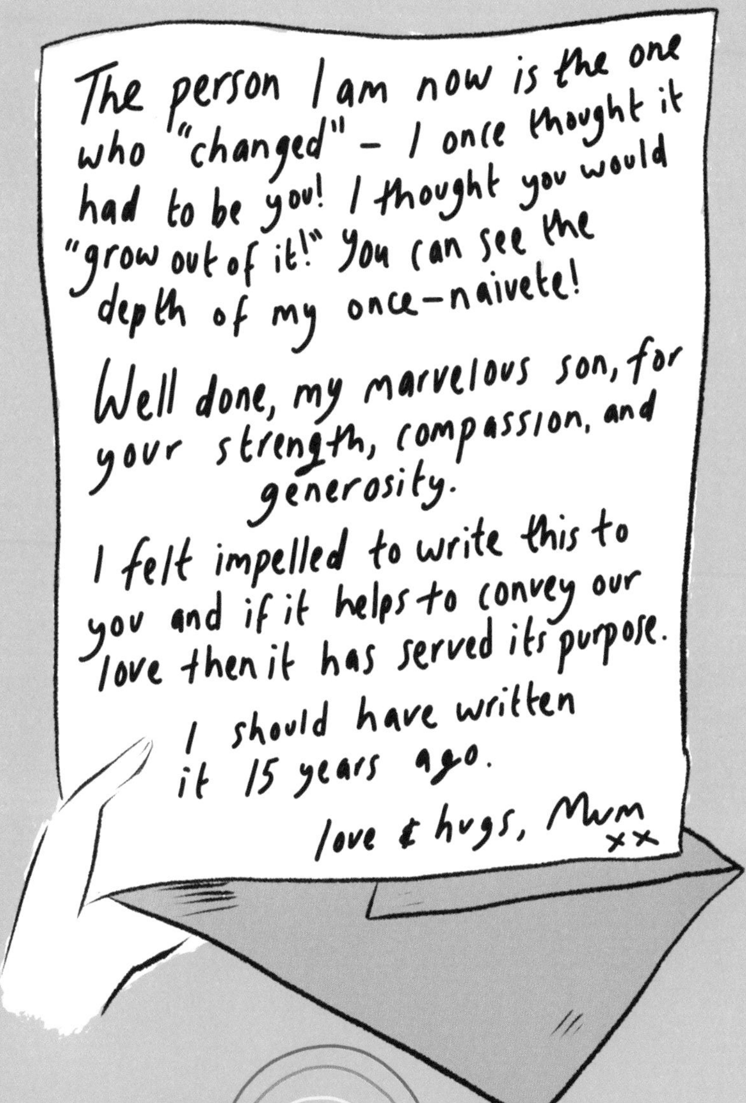

The person I am now is the one
who "changed" — I once thought it
had to be you! I thought you would
"grow out of it!" You can see the
depth of my once-naivete!

Well done, my marvelous son, for
your strength, compassion, and
generosity.

I felt impelled to write this to
you and if it helps to convey our
love then it has served its purpose.

I should have written
it 15 years ago.

love & hugs, Mum
xx

Chapter 6

RAINBOW WORDS

LLY - A (typically) straight and/or cis person who supports members of the LGBTQ+ community.

 SEXUAL (OR ACE) - Someone who does not experience sexual attraction.

 I/BISEXUAL - Refers to an emotional, romantic, and/or sexual orientation toward more than one gender.

 IPHOBIA - The fear or dislike of someone who identifies as bi based on prejudice or negative attitudes, beliefs, or views about bi people. Biphobic bullying may be targeted at people who are, or who are perceived to be, bi.

 ISGENDER OR CIS - Someone whose gender identity is the same as the sex they were assigned at birth. Non-trans is also used by some people.

 OMING OUT - When a person first tells someone/others about their identity as lesbian, gay, bi, or trans.

 EADNAMING - Calling someone by their birth name after they have changed their name. This term is often associated with trans people who have changed their name as part of their transition.

 AY- Refers to a man who has an emotional, romantic, and/or sexual orientation toward men. Also a generic term for lesbian and gay sexuality—some women define themselves as gay rather than lesbian.

 ENDER - Often expressed in terms of masculinity and femininity, gender is largely culturally determined and is assumed from the sex assigned at birth.

-173-

ENDER DYSPHORIA - Used to describe when a person experiences discomfort or distress because there is a mismatch between their sex assigned at birth and their gender identity. This is also the clinical diagnosis for someone who doesn't feel comfortable with the gender they were assigned at birth.

ENDER EXPRESSION - How a person chooses to outwardly express their gender, within the context of societal expectations of gender. A person who does not conform to societal expectations of gender may not, however, identify as trans.

ENDER IDENTITY - A person's innate sense of their own gender, whether male, female, or something else (see NON-BINARY), which may or may not correspond to the sex assigned at birth.

ENDER REASSIGNMENT - Another way of describing a person's transition. To undergo gender reassignment usually means to undergo some sort of medical intervention, but it can also mean changing names, pronouns, dressing differently, and living in their self-identified gender.

ETEROSEXUAL / STRAIGHT - Refers to a man who has an emotional, romantic, and/or sexual orientation toward women or to a woman who has an emotional, romantic, and/or sexual orientation toward men.

OMOSEXUAL - This might be considered a more medical term used to describe someone who has an emotional, romantic, and/or sexual orientation toward someone of the same gender. The term "gay" is now more generally used.

OMOPHOBIA - The fear or dislike of someone, based on prejudice or negative attitudes, beliefs, or views about lesbian, gay, or bi people. Homophobic bullying may be targeted at people who are, or who are perceived to be, lesbian, gay, or bi.

NTERSEX - A term used to describe a person who may have the biological attributes of both sexes or whose biological attributes do not fit with societal assumptions about what constitutes male or female. Intersex people may identify as male, female, or non-binary.

GBT - The acronym for lesbian, gay, bi, and trans.

LESBIAN - Refers to a woman who has an emotional, romantic, and/or sexual orientation toward women.

NEURODIVERSE - A concept where neurological differences are recognized and respected in the same way as any other human difference.

NONBINARY - An umbrella term for a person who does not identify as only male or female, or who may identify as both.

OUTED - When a lesbian, gay, bi, or trans person's sexual orientation or gender identity is disclosed to someone else without their consent.

PERSON WITH A TRANS HISTORY - Someone who identifies as male or female or a man or woman but was assigned differently at birth. This is increasingly used by people to acknowledge a trans past.

PANSEXUAL - Refers to a person whose emotional, romantic, and/or sexual attraction toward others is not limited by sex or gender.

PASSING - If someone is regarded, at a glance, to be a cisgender man or cisgender woman. Cisgender refers to someone whose gender identity matches the sex they were assigned at birth. This might include physical gender cues (hair or clothing) and/or behavior that is historically or culturally associated with a particular gender.

PRONOUN - Words we use to refer to people's gender in conversation—for example, "he" or "she." Some people may prefer others to refer to them in gender-neutral language and use pronouns such as they/their and ze/zir.

QUEER - In the past a derogatory term for LGBT individuals. The term has now been reclaimed by LGBT young people in particular who don't identify with traditional categories around gender identity and sexual orientation, but the term is still viewed to be derogatory by some.

QUESTIONING - The process of exploring your own sexual orientation and/or gender identity.

SEX - Assigned to a person on the basis of primary sex characteristics (genitalia) and reproductive functions. Sometimes the terms "sex" and "gender" are interchanged to mean "male" or "female."

EXUAL ORIENTATION - A person's emotional, romantic, and/or sexual attraction to another person.

RANS - An umbrella term to describe people whose gender is not the same as, or does not sit comfortably with, the sex they were assigned at birth. Trans people may describe themselves using one or more of a wide variety of terms, including (but not limited to) transgender, transsexual, gender-queer (GQ), genderfluid, non-binary, gender-variant, crossdresser, genderless, agender, nongender, third gender, two-spirit, bi-gender, trans man, trans woman, trans masculine, trans feminine, and neutrois.

RANSGENDER MAN - A term used to describe someone who is assigned female at birth but identifies and lives as a man. This may be shortened to trans man, or FTM, an abbreviation for female-to-male.

RANSGENDER WOMAN - A term used to describe someone who is assigned male at birth but identifies and lives as a woman. This may be shortened to trans woman, or MTF, an abbreviation for male-to-female.

RANSITIONING - The steps a trans person may take to live in the gender with which they identify. Each person's transition will involve different things. For some this involves medical intervention, such as hormone therapy and surgeries, but not all trans people want or are able to have this. Transitioning also might involve things such as telling friends and family, dressing differently, and changing official documents.

RANSPHOBIA - The fear or dislike of someone based on the fact they are trans, including the denial/refusal to accept their gender identity.

RANSSEXUAL - This was used in the past as a more medical term (similarly to homosexual) to refer to someone who transitioned to live in the "opposite" gender to the one assigned at birth. This term is still used by some, although many people prefer the term trans or transgender.

THANK YOU!

This book would not have happened without a ton of amazing human beings who have really helped me put this together and get it out there!

To Maryann, Megan, Luca, and Jay, Alex, and Beth from Inclusive Minds, and their Inclusion Ambassadors network for connecting us, and Halimah from Penguin Random House, for reading through this book and giving me the feedback I needed to make this the most inclusive, fun, and accessible book I could, for readers from all walks of life!

To Carmen and Natalie at Penguin Random House, for being a great pair of Peng-Kween editors and embracing this book with open arms and a great pair of rainbow jeans. Thank you for taking on this huge project without worry and embracing it with so much love and care, while also listening to my ideas and being open to a rainbow llamacorn.

To Emily, your design work on the inside and cover is amazing. Thank you for taking care of so many jobs and doing so many cool things with InDesign that I would have no idea how to do. You are da best!

To my amazing Penguin Workshop team who have really helped me craft this book into the cutest USA format, THANK YOU SO MUCH. Don't know what I would have done without you on this. So Rob, Kayla, Francesco, and the team, you slay! And to my favorite US Spice Girls, Karli J (Karl) and Gabbi, I genuinely appreciate and am so thankful for all your passion, love, and involvement on this edition of the book. It really means a lot to me.

To MNEK and Juno Dawson, huge thanks for giving me exclusive quotes that will resonate with readers across the globe, and to Jade Thirlwall for putting up with countless DMs of me trying to figure out the best quote for you when we realized it was on Insta all along and just needed a rainbow cowboy hat to complete the look.

I didn't realize how much I needed a Lauren till I met a Lauren. LG, you are THE best literary agent out there and I'm so thankful for you. Without you, this book wouldn't have been in front of the right people. Every day I'm so proud to say you represent me and I'm so thankful for your ability to translate my idea ramblings into everyday wording. #TeamSassy

To all my mates who have put up with countless WhatsApps, canceled plans and no-shows due to me working on this book. Totally worth it, though! Thank you for being the best crew I could surround myself with. You empower me so much. I love ya.

Finally, to my brilliant and brave family, Mum, Dad, and Anne-Marie. We have come a VERY long way since those early days of me coming out, and I am so so proud of YOU for letting me tell OUR story to help others. We're a very, very small family, but we're so lucky to have each other. You are my own personal rainbow.

HELPLINE BLING

Whenever (if ever) you decide to come out, it's something that needs to be done safely.
Remember to take your time—don't rush yourself, and if you're not ready to reach out to somebody you know, then these helplines are available:

The Trevor Project
An LGBTQ+ Crisis Intervention & Suicide Prevention Organization
1-866-488-7386
www.thetrevorproject.org

Trans Lifeline
A Peer-Support Crisis Hotline
1-877-565-8860
www.translifeline.org

STONEWALL
The LGBT
Equality Charity
www.stonewall.org.uk

CREDITS

Page 9 - lyrics from the song "We All Try," written by Frank Ocean and Happy Perez

Page 16 - quote from Nanette, written and performed by Hannah Gadsby

Page 26 - quote from Jonathan Van Ness, Queer Eye, season 2

Page 37 - quote from Courtney Act, RuPaul's Drag Race: Untucked, season 6

Page 54 - quote from Adam Rippon in his speech on accepting the Human Rights Campaign's Visibility Award

Page 59 - quote from Ellen DeGeneres on Twitter

Page 62 - quote from Juno Dawson, exclusive to FREE TO BE ME

Page 76 - quote from Lady Gaga on Instagram

Page 81 - extract from "The Next Chapter," a blog post written by Robbie Rogers

Page 85 - quote from Sylvia Rivera

Page 105 - extract from "Dear Men of 'The Breakfast Club': Trans Women Aren't a Prop, Ploy, or Sexual Predators," an open letter to radio show The Breakfast Club, written by Janet Mock

Page 108 - quote from Lena Waithe from her acceptance speech at the Emmy Awards 2017

Page 114 - quote from Cher in an interview on The Graham Norton Show

Page 121 - quote from Harvey Milk from "The Hope Speech" given in 1978

Page 122 - extract from From a Land Where Other People Live by Audre Lorde, published in 1973

Page 122 - quote from Freddie Mercury during a live show in 1985

Page 123 - quote from Bayard Rustin

Page 124 - quote from Marsha P. Johnson

Page 127 - extract from "I was banned from prom for dressing in drag—now my story is a West End musical," an article published on www.bbc.co.uk, written by Jamie Campbell

Page 142 - quote from MNEK, exclusive to FREE TO BE ME

Page 146 - quote from Aaron Philip in an interview with Paper magazine

Page 165 - quote from Kenny Ethan Jones from ShortList interview